ABRAHAM JOSHUA HESCHEL

Man of Spirit,
Man of Action

To Marty,
A pleasure to share this
book with you!

Best,

~~~signature~~~ . זלק

OR N. ROSE

THE JEWISH PUBLICATION SOCIETY
Philadelphia   2003/5763

The Jewish Publication Society
2100 Arch Street, 2ⁿᵈ floor
Phildelphia, PA 19103

The following photographs were previously published in Edward K. Kaplan and Samuel H. Dresner, *Abraham Joshua Heschel, Prophetic Witness* (New Haven, London: Yale University Press, 1998), pages 24, 25, 26, 27, 28, 29; Edward K. Kaplan, *Holiness in Words, Abraham Joshua Heschel's Poetics of Piety* (Albany, NY: State University of New York Press, 1996), pages 31 (bottom), 33 (top), 37, 38.

Design and Composition by Book Design Studio II

Manufactured in the United States of America

03 04 05 06 07 08 09 10   10 9 8 7 6 5 4 3 2 1

Library of Congress Cataloging-in-Publication Data
Rose, Or N.
   Abraham Joshua Heschel : man of spirit, man of action / Or Rose.—1st ed.
      p. cm.
Includes index.
Summary: Profiles Abraham Heschel, a Jewish rabbi who grew up in eastern Europe, taught, spoke, and wrote about Judaism and civil rights; and walked with Martin Luther King, Jr., in the 1965 march in Selma, Alabama.
   ISBN 0-9276-0758-X
   1. Heschel, Abraham Joshua, 1907–1972. 2. Rabbis—United States—Biography—Juvenile literature. 3. Jewish scholars—United States—Biography—Juvenile literature. [1. Heschel, Abraham Joshua, 1907–1972. 2. Rabbis. 3. Civil rights workers. 4. Jews—Biography.] I. Title.
   BM755.H37R67 2003
   296.3'092—dc21
                                    2003009990

CONTENTS

Publication of this book is made with the support of
Alan B. Slifka,
father of David Slifka, Class of 1993,
The Abraham Joshua Heschel School, New York City,
in memory of
Rabbi Marshall T. Meyer and Rabbi Eugene Weiner
who were touched by the sparks of their association with
Rabbi Abraham Joshua Heschel
and in honor of
the board, faculty, and administration of
The Abraham Joshua Heschel School, New York City,
who are likewise enriched by their devotion to and admiration of Rabbi Heschel

and

Rabbi Jonathan Lipnick and
Susan C. Scheuer

and

is dedicated
in loving memory of
Ezra and Sylvia Shapiro,
who taught by example
the importance of tikkun olam,
by Catharyn and Mike Gildesgame

ACKNOWLEDGMENTS

I would like to thank the following people
for their help in completing this project:
Sylvia and Susannah Heschel,
Ellen Frankel, Carol Hupping, Christine Sweeney,
Tina Espy, Robin Norman, and the entire JPS staff,
Peter Geffen, Edward Kaplan, Arthur and Kathy Green,
Yossi Abramowitz, Joel Grishaver, Sylvia Fuks-Fried,
Yonina Dorph, Sheldon and Gail Dorph,
Joyce Klein, Ebn Leader, Tamara Gropper, Zev Shanken,
Jonny Mars, Liza Elkin, and Judith Rosenbaum.

To my colleagues and students at
the Abraham Joshua Heschel School of Manhattan,
the Park Avenue Synagogue, and
the Jewish Community Day School—*Todah rabbah!*

To my parents

Rabbi Neal and Carol Rose

My first teachers of Torah

"She speaks words of wisdom

and a teaching of kindness is on his lips."

(based on Proverbs 31:26)

FOREWORD

My father loved being a father. And he was a wonderful father. When I remember him, I think most of all about his tenderness and his exuberance. He was full of affection and he loved to show it. When I was little, he invented games for me, played "zoo," even tried to take an interest in my paper dolls. As I grew older, he was my source of comfort and understanding, sympathizing with the pains of adolescence. Whenever he came home from his office, or I interrupted him while he was working, he threw open his arms and exclaimed, "Susie!"

Joy and excitement filled our home as soon as my father came home from work. He was anxious to share the news of his day, ready to play hide-and-seek with me, enthusiastic for the dinner my mother had prepared. After dinner, we frequently played "school" in the living room, with my parents pretending to be the pupils while I was the teacher. We had a hilarious reenactment of my day at school, and my father loved to take the role of one of the mischievous little boys in my class.

My parents created a home imbued with the spirit that my father describes in his books. The Sabbath and Jewish holidays were days of celebration, but also times of holiness. We sometimes had guests for dinner, or for tea on Shabbat afternoons, and the conversations inevitably turned to memories of Europe. Nearly all of my parents' friends were refugee scholars, and years after the war, they remained in shock at what had happened. Other times, my father would talk about Hasidic *rebbes*, telling us stories and teachings of his ancestors.

My father's legacy is enormous. To scholars he has given remarkable insights into Jewish theology, to religious people he has given a language to communicate across divisions. To me, as his only child, he gave a vision of the extraordinary heights of love and compassion a human being can reach.

Susannah Heschel
Eli Black Associate Professor of Jewish Studies
Dartmouth College

INTRODUCTION

"I have learned from the prophets
that I have to be involved in the affairs of man,
in the affairs of suffering man."

March 21, 1965, was one of the most important days in American history. The Reverend Martin Luther King Jr. organized a massive civil rights demonstration of 30,000 people in Selma, Alabama. The marchers took to the streets demanding that local government officials allow African Americans* to vote. Although the U.S. government had extended this right to African Americans long ago, there were still many racist politicians and policemen who tried to stop them from getting to the voting booths.

The Reverend King invited a small group of religious and political leaders to join him on the front lines of this historic march. One of these people was his good friend Abraham Joshua Heschel.

---

* Like other groups of people, African Americans have been called by different names at different times in history. During the 1950 and1960s, they were often called Negroes (as Rabbi Heschel called them). In the 1970s, the term Afro-American was introduced in place of Negro. Today, the term African American is considered the preferred term by members of this community and by those speaking or writing about them.

Rabbi Heschel was an extraordinary Jewish teacher, who taught the values of justice and compassion through his words *and* his actions.

As he walked arm-in-arm with the other civil rights leaders, Heschel was easy to spot in the crowd. He looked like a prophet from the Bible: he had long white hair, a bushy beard, and wore a large *kippah* on his head. Like the Hebrew prophets of old, Rabbi Heschel believed that standing up for the rights of others was a religious obligation. As he once wrote, "I have learned from the prophets that I have to be involved in the affairs of man, in the affairs of suffering man."

Abraham Joshua Heschel first learned the values of justice and compassion as a child in his home in Eastern Europe.

1

The Heschel Home

*"I was very fortunate in having lived as a child . . .
in an environment where there were many people . . .
concerned with problems of the inner life,
of spirituality and integrity . . . people who have shown
great compassion and understanding for other people."*

Abraham Joshua Heschel was born on January 11, 1907 in
Warsaw, Poland. He was the descendent of seven genera-
tions of Hasidic masters—charismatic rabbis and teachers who led Jewish communities throughout Eastern
Europe. His father, Moshe Mordechai, was a Hasidic master. His mother, Rivka Reizel, was the daughter and the
twin sister of Hasidic masters. Abraham Joshua's parents
expected that he, too, would become a Hasidic master
some day.

Abraham Joshua was the youngest of six children. He
had four sisters: Sarah Brakha, Esther Sima, Gittel, and
Devorah Miriam, and one brother, Jacob. Avremele ("little
Abraham" in Yiddish) was the darling of the family. He
was pampered and fussed over by his brother and sisters.

The Heschels lived in a small apartment attached to the neighborhood *shteibel* (small prayer house and study hall) at 40 Muranowska Street, in the heart of Hasidic Warsaw. This was where Abraham Joshua's father worked as a rabbi, teaching the members of his community the wisdom of the Jewish tradition and guiding them in their day-to-day lives.

Moshe Mordechai was the leader of a very poor community and was paid only a small salary. Abraham Joshua's mother did not work outside of the house; she was responsible for the care of her children and for the upkeep of the Heschel home.

Life was not easy for the Heschels. Abraham Joshua had to share a tiny bedroom with his brother, and many of his clothes were hand-me-downs from older friends and relatives. Nonetheless, the Heschel home was a place of great love and warmth. Their most prized treasures were not silver or gold, but ancient religious teachings and folktales, and wordless melodies and simple dances. In fact, the Heschels had an extraordinary family tradition: each night after dinner, the whole family would gather any money left in the house, and Abraham Joshua's father would give it away to the poorest people in the community.

2

Magical Adventures

"Many Jews talked about God, but it was the Ba'al Shem Tov who brought God to the people."

While Abraham Joshua grew up in Warsaw, the biggest city in all of Eastern Europe, he always felt a special connection to a tiny Ukrainian village called Mezbizh. To an outsider, this quiet country town, with its dirt roads and small cottage homes, would not look very interesting. However, Abraham Joshua's father was born in Mezbizh, and he told his son some amazing stories about his boyhood village.

"Come sit on my knee, Avremele, and join me on a magical journey to Mezbizh!"

Abraham Joshua climbed onto his father's lap, closed his eyes, and imagined that he was actually sitting in a horse-drawn carriage bound for the Ukraine!

"Welcome to Mezbizh, my son. Today we are making only one stop. We are visiting the home of the Ba'al Shem

Tov—the first Hasidic master and one of the greatest teachers in our tradition!"

"What was so great about him?" asked Abraham Joshua.

"He discovered the secret," whispered Moshe Mordechai, ". . . the secret of the hidden sparks."

"Hidden sparks . . . ," Abraham Joshua repeated with great curiosity.

"Yes," said Moshe Mordechai. "The Ba'al Shem Tov taught that there are hidden sparks of holiness inside of every creation."

Abraham Joshua's eyes widened as he searched the room for these mysterious sparks. Moshe Mordechai let out a loud laugh. "Oy, my precious boy, you can't find the sparks by simply widening your eyes. You must search for them with an open heart. If you look for the good in all people and all things, then God's light will shine through. The Ba'al Shem Tov said that even the smallest blade of grass has a holy spark."

"Please, Tateh (Father), tell me more!"

"Many years after the death of the Ba'al Shem Tov," Moshe Mordechai continued, "another great teacher came to Mezbizh. He was so extraordinary that some folks actually thought that the Ba'al Shem Tov had come back to life!"

"Who was this amazing person?" Abraham Joshua wanted to know.

"I am proud to tell you that he was your great, great-grandfather, the first Abraham Joshua Heschel."

"He was the man I was named after!" said Abraham Joshua with great excitement.

"Exactly!" answered Moshe Mordechai.

"Like the Ba'al Shem Tov, Zeide (Grandfather) Heschel also knew the secret of the holy sparks. He had the special gift of being able to uncover the good in every person he met. He even treated the simple water carriers and wood-choppers of Mezbizh with love and respect. Our Zeide was so well known for his kind ways that he was given the nickname, Ohev Yisroel, the one who loves all of the people of Israel."

Abraham Joshua's father hugged his young son. "My boy, you have been given a very special name, and when you are old enough, you too will lead your people with love and respect. You see, every generation needs an Abraham Joshua Heschel."

3

A Hasidic Prince

*"I have one talent and that is the capacity to be
tremendously surprised, surprised by life. . . .
This is to me the supreme Hasidic imperative [command]."*

As a child, Abraham Joshua was treated like a prince (a
poor prince, but a prince, nonetheless) by the members of
his Hasidic community. The Hasidim respected his father
and they were dedicated to the teachings of the Ba'al
Shem Tov and the Ohev Yisroel. They showed their loy-
alty to the Heschels by treating every member of the family, even the littlest one, with great honor. When Abraham
Joshua entered his father's *shteibel*, the Hasidim leaped
out of their seats to make room for him. When he walked
through the neighborhood, people of all ages stood in respect and greeted him as he passed by, *"Shalom aleikhem*,
Peace be with you, little Heschel!"

Soon, however, Abraham Joshua was recognized not
only as a member of the famous Heschel family, but also
because of his own gifts—his own inner sparks. Once,
while visiting with his best friend Yechiel Hoffer, at the

Hoffer Family Fabric Store, Abraham Joshua amazed everyone there by quietly memorizing the color, size, style, and price of all of the fabrics in the store! "Blue, purple, green; cotton, wool, linen," he could be heard saying, as his friend Yechiel looked on, making sure that Heschel was not peeking. By age six, Abraham Joshua had been identified by his teachers as an *illui* (a genius). At school, they would raise him onto a desk at the front of the class-room and quiz him on little-known facts about Jewish life. As Abraham Joshua sat atop the wooden table, his little legs dangling over the edge, students of all ages crowded around him, waiting to hear what he would say next!

But it was not just Abraham Joshua's gifted mind that made him so special; it was also his *neshamah*, his caring spirit. When Abraham Joshua was seven years old, he studied the terrifying story of the Binding of Isaac for the first time. As his teacher read aloud from the Bible, Abra-ham Joshua sat attentively, listening to every word, anx-iously waiting to hear how things were going to turn out.

"And at the last possible moment," said the rabbi, "an angel came forth from the skies and saved young Isaac and his father from disaster."

At that instant, Abraham Joshua began to cry uncon-trollably. The rabbi, confused by Abraham Joshua's reac-tion, closed his book and turned to his sad student.

"Why are you weeping, child? Don't you understand, Isaac was saved?" Tears still streaming down his face, Abraham Joshua replied, "But Rabbi, suppose the angel had come just a second too late?"

Touched by his student's compassion, the teacher put his arm around Avremele and said to him, "Angels are never late."

4

A Time of Sadness

*"My father used to tell me a story about our grandfather,
the Ohev Israel. He was asked by many rebbes
[Hasidic rabbis], 'How come your prayers are
always answered, and ours are not?'
He gave the following answer:
'You see, whenever some Jew comes to me
and pours out his heart . . . I have such compassion
that a little hole is created in my heart. . . .
I take my heart and place it before God.
He sees this broken heart. He has compassion for
my heart. . . . He listens to my prayers."*

In the winter of 1916, a dark shadow fell over the Heschel
home. Abraham Joshua's father died, just six weeks before
his son's tenth birthday. Avremele was heartbroken. He
wished that he could have heard his Tateh's sweet voice
as he told just one more magical Mezbizh tale.

With the loss of Moshe Mordechai, Abraham Joshua's
mother had to take full responsibility for her family. Not
only did she care for her children and the home, but she
also tended to the *shteibel*, so that her husband's followers
would still have a special place to study and pray. Rela-

9

tives did all they could to help the Heschels, but times were tough. Everyone in the Heschel home had to help out, even Abraham Joshua. He pitched in by going with his big brother, Jacob, to sell matches and other small trinkets in the local market.

One person who was especially helpful to Abraham Joshua during this difficult time was his mother's twin brother, Rabbi Israel Shimon Perlow, known in the Hasidic world as the Master from Novominsk. Uncle Israel was a kind and generous man, but he was also very strict. He believed that life was a gift from God and not a single moment of it should be wasted. So, each morning he awoke at sunrise, prayed, studied, and worked all day long, taking only two short breaks for meals: lunch at exactly two o'clock in the afternoon and dinner at midnight.

Uncle Israel loved Abraham Joshua very much and treated him like a son, even though he already had twelve children of his own. The Novominsker saw great promise in his nephew; he was sure that Abraham Joshua was going to be the next great Hasidic master in Warsaw. "Someday soon," Uncle Israel would say, "you will take your rightful place as the leader of this holy community."

The Novominsker made it his mission to mold Avremele into a Hasidic master. He even paid for a private tutor to live with Abraham Joshua, so that he could study day and night. In exchange, Uncle Israel demanded a great deal from his nephew. Unlike other children his age, Abraham Joshua was not given much time to play with friends. Sometimes, this made him sad. However, he also knew that if he wanted to become a Hasidic master, like the other great men in his family, he would have to work very hard.

5

Finding God in Unexpected Places

*"God is hiding in the world and our task is
to let the Divine [God] emerge from our deeds."*

Abraham Joshua continued to develop into a fine master-in-training. When he was only fourteen years old, he wrote a series of articles for a magazine called *Gates of Torah*. Everyone in Hasidic Warsaw assumed that he was on his way to becoming the next great leader of the community. "When Avremele becomes a *rebbe*," people would say, "none of the other masters will have any followers left." Some folks even started to give Abraham Joshua *kvitelah* (little notes with their prayers on them), believing that he had a special connection to God and could help them have their prayers answered!

But by the time Abraham Joshua was fifteen, he was thinking new thoughts and dreaming of a different future for himself. He was no longer a child, but a young man full of curiosity and wonder. And lately, he had been more interested in subjects like poetry and art than the usual things studied by the Hasidic masters. In fact, at his school students were allowed to study these nonreligious subjects for only a few hours a week. Abraham Joshua's teachers felt that delving too deeply into these topics was dangerous. They said it was distracting and would lead young people away from the Jewish tradition.

Abraham Joshua ignored these warnings and began exploring the subjects he loved outside of school. He felt that people should be able to study whatever interested them. "After all," said Heschel, "wasn't it the Ba'al Shem Tov, the greatest of all the Hasidic masters, who taught that God's holy light is present in all things?"

Abraham Joshua started his new adventure without telling his uncle or his mother, knowing that they would disapprove of his decision. Instead, he went to cafés and libraries in other Warsaw neighborhoods to read books and talk with poets and philosophers. People were always surprised to see a young Hasid with *peiyis* (side locks) and traditional Hasidic clothing sitting in such places. But Abraham Joshua did not let that stop him; he quietly continued his adventures, all the while keeping his secret from his family.

But this would not last for long.

6

From Warsaw to Vilna

*"Vilna stood the at center of Eastern European Jewish life
. . . [it was] the meeting place of poets, philosophers
and religious seekers. . . ."*

One evening, when Abraham Joshua was sixteen years old, he sat down at the living room table to read. When his mother came in, she noticed something strange. She saw her son looking at a large Hebrew book but heard him reading quietly in Polish. When she took a closer look, she realized exactly what he was up to. Abraham Joshua had hidden a small Polish book between the pages of his Bible!

Rivka Reizel was shocked. A thousand questions raced through her mind at once. Why was her Avremele keeping this secret from her? Did he want to give up the Jewish tradition for the modern world, like so many young people had done recently? She took a deep breath, gathered her thoughts, and confronted her son.

"Avremele, I know what you are doing. It is time for us to talk."

At first, Abraham Joshua was embarrassed and scared. After months of hiding his secret from his family he had been caught, and his mother looked angry and disappointed. However, he was also relieved, because he could finally share his true feelings with her.

"Mamme, I love the Torah (the teachings of the Jewish tradition) and the teachings of the Hasidic masters, but I need more. I want to study art, math, poetry, and philosophy. I want to leave Warsaw and go to the modern Jewish high school in Vilna."

Abraham Joshua's mother saw the pain on her son's face and understood that he had been unhappy for some time. After many discussions with Uncle Israel and other relatives, she agreed to let Abraham Joshua go to Vilna, in Lithuania. The Heschel family was sad to see him leave; they loved their Avremele and were going to miss him very much. They were also sad because they knew that he might never become the great Hasidic master that everyone hoped he would be.

It was on a Saturday night, after the close of the Sabbath, that Abraham Joshua changed his special, black, velvet *Shabbos* (Sabbath) hat for an ordinary weekday cap and set out on his journey to Vilna. Many friends and relatives came to say good-bye to him at the train station. Just moments before he left, Abraham Joshua's teacher—the one who had taught him the story of the Binding of Isaac—came running up to Abraham Joshua and asked to speak with him privately.

"Avremele," his teacher said, still catching his breath, "no matter how far you travel from home, always remember the teaching of the hidden sparks. Care for the light that is within you and search for it wherever you go."

With these words in his heart, seventeen-year-old Abraham Joshua left for Vilna.

7

The Birth of a Poet

"When I wander through boulevards of poetry . . .
I whisper secrets to that space in which
my mysteries reside. . . ."

At his new school, Heschel met Jewish students from all over Eastern Europe; some were religious but many more were not. As a boy, the only friends he had were the children in his Hasidic neighborhood, and because of his busy study schedule, he rarely had time to play with them. Though he was a shy person, Abraham—as his schoolmates now called him—soon made new friends with people from all walks of life. Together with his friends, he helped create a club for young Jewish artists and writers called Young Vilna.

As a teenager in Warsaw, Abraham had written several essays on Jewish law. Now, as a young adult in Vilna, he tried his hand at poetry. Most of his poems were about God, friends, and nature.

Open,
open your friendship to me

there is so much room for you
your entire world can fit in my open, spread out arms.

Abraham dedicated his first book of poetry to his father's memory.

While Abraham no longer dressed like a Hasid or studied only religious books, he remained observant of Jewish law and proud of his heritage. He lived with an elderly religious man on the outskirts of Vilna, and he often took the long train ride home to Warsaw to visit his family. And as his old schoolteacher had instructed, he never forgot about the holy sparks.

On a cool spring day in Vilna, Abraham set out for a long walk with his friend Shlomo. As the two young men approached the magnificent forest at the edge of the city, Abraham surprised Shlomo by reaching into his knapsack for a hat. While Shlomo knew that his friend had been raised in a Hasidic home, where men wore dark clothing and hats, he also knew that it was Abraham's personal custom to cover his head only at special times, such as when he studied Torah or entered a synagogue. But to put on a hat now, at the edge of the forest, seemed strange.

"Abraham, what are you doing? Why are you putting on a hat now of all times?" asked Shlomo.

Heschel gently raised his hands to the sky and answered his friend. "I have learned from the Hasidic masters that a forest is a holy place, and I do not enter any holy place without first covering my head. When I feel the warmth of the sun shining on my face, I feel blessed; when I smell the fresh scent of the trees or crumble the crisp leaves between my fingers, I know that God's holy light surrounds me. All of these living things are like traces of God's footprints."

8

Berlin: Faith Challenged, Faith Rediscovered

*"As civilization advances, the sense of wonder declines.
Mankind will not perish for want [lack] of information,
but only for want of appreciation. . . . Life without wonder
is not worth living."*

After graduating from high school in Vilna, Abraham traveled to Berlin, Germany, to begin his university studies. At the time, Berlin was the great center of modern life in Europe; it was even bigger and more exciting than Warsaw. There were many universities, museums, concert halls, theaters, and sporting events. Berlin also had excellent schools for Jewish studies. Twenty-year-old Abraham was very excited to begin his adult life in such an interesting city.

Abraham enrolled at the University of Berlin, where he studied philosophy and art history. He also trained to become a modern rabbi—using the wisdom of the Torah along with many new ideas from secular sources to guide the European Jewish community. Abraham was busy studying day and night. He loved to learn, but was often frustrated because none of his professors appreciated the teaching of the holy sparks. In fact, most of them thought that his ideas about God and religion were old-fashioned and silly. He was beginning to question his own beliefs.

After finishing a long and exhausting day at the university, Abraham decided to take a relaxing walk home. As he strolled through the magnificent streets of Berlin, he thought about the day's lessons and how confused he had been feeling of late. Then suddenly, he was distracted from his thoughts by the sunset. The sun's soft rays sparkled and danced off the cobblestone streets, and the sky looked like someone had just painted it with bright streaks of orange, red, and purple.

"What an amazing sight," Heschel said to himself, as the sun dipped gently below the horizon. Suddenly, a chill ran down his spine and a thought flashed through his mind: "I have been so worried about my university studies and the opinions of my professors that I almost forgot about the holy sparks. This sunset has reminded me of my true beliefs: only God could have created something as magical as this; and I want to dedicate my life to helping other people discover God's holy sparks in creation."

Abraham looked up into the night sky and began chanting the ancient words of the evening prayer:

Blessed Are You, God, Creator of the universe,
Who by Your word brings on the evening twilight.

9

The Flames of the Holocaust

*"Human life is holy,
holier even than the scrolls of the Torah."*

Unfortunately, Abraham was living at a time in history when many Germans were not able to recognize the holy sparks in all people. A dark cloud of hatred hovered over the entire country. Adolf Hitler, leader of the Nazi political party and a vicious anti-Semite (hater of Jews), had just come to power. He claimed that Jews and other minorities were responsible for all the problems in Germany. Hitler said that life in Germany would be perfect if only these "outsiders" were removed from society. Sadly, far too many Germans believed Hitler's twisted lies, and his spirit of hatred spread like wildfire.

First, Jews were made to feel like outsiders at work and at school. They were paid less money than other German workers and were ignored by their teachers. When Abraham first arrived at the University of Berlin, many professors liked him and thought that he was a promising student. Now, these same people treated him like a complete stranger. Life at the university became so difficult for Abraham that he was forced to wait three extra years to graduate, simply because he was a Jew. No one would read his papers or grade his exams. Heschel would never forget how painful and lonely it felt to be treated like a dreaded outsider.

While struggling to complete his university studies, Abraham began to teach at the same school where he had recently finished his training as a modern rabbi. He also started to write books on Torah and philosophy, and began giving speeches against Hitler's terrible actions. In the spring of 1933, when the Nazis organized a public book burning at the university, he wrote a poem entitled "On the Day of Hate." Heschel described how the city of Berlin looked like a "volcano" as thousands of Jewish holy books were removed from libraries and burned in a huge public bonfire.

Once, while studying at a small library owned by a group of German priests, Abraham asked the librarians why they had not spoken out against the cruelty of the Nazis. "After all," said Heschel, "the Bible teaches us that everyone is created in the image of God!" Surprised by Abraham's statement, the head librarian replied with a puzzled look on his face, "Yes, but if we speak out against the Nazis, they will close our library, and then all of these precious books will be lost to the world." Abraham was so shocked by this unfeeling response that he began to tremble. The book he was holding fell from his hands and dropped to the floor. Paying no attention to the fallen book, Abraham looked deep into the eyes of the librarian and asked, "How can you possibly measure the value of books against human life?"

Within a short period of time, the flames of Hitler's hatred spread throughout much of Europe. From 1933 to 1945, anti-Semitism was the official law of the land in Germany and the other countries that it conquered during the Second World War. Millions of Jews and other minorities were forced from their homes and made to live in filthy, cramped places called ghettos and concentration camps, where they were tortured and often murdered. This terrible period of history is known as the Holocaust. The violent flames of the Holocaust were the exact opposite of the holy sparks that the Ba'al Shem Tov had spoken of so long ago.

Heschel's father, Rabbi Moshe Mordechai Heschel, and his mother, Rivka Reizel Heschel. (Courtesy of Yitzhak Meir Twersky and Thena Heshel Kendall)

Heschel's sister, Sarah Brakha Heschel and brother, Jacob Heshel.
(Courtesy of Yitzhak Meir Twersky and Thena Heshel Kendall)

Heschel's sisters (clockwise, from top left), Devorah Miriam Dermer, Gittel Heschel and Esther Sima Heschel. (Courtesy of Yitzhak Meir Twersky and Thena Heshel Kendall)

Young Heschel in Warsaw, about age seventeen. (Courtesy of Yitzhak Meir Twersky and Thena Heshel Kendall)

QVOD FELIX FAVSTVMQVE SIT

VNIVERSITATIS LITTERARIAE
FRIDERICAE GVILELMAE
BEROLINENSIS

RECTORE MAGNIFICO

WILHELM KRUEGER

MEDICINAE VETERINARIAE DOCTORE IN HAC VNIVERSITATE ANATOMIAE VETERINARIAE PROFESSORE
PVBLICO ORDINARIO

EX DECRETO ORDINIS AMPLISSIMI PHILOSOPHORVM
PROMOTOR LEGITIME CONSTITVTVS

LUDWIG BIEBERBACH

PHILOSOPHIAE DOCTOR IN HAC VNIVERSITATE PROFESSOR PVBLICVS ORDINARIVS
ACADEMIAE SCIENTIARVM BORVSSICAE SOCIVS

ORDINIS PHILOSOPHORVM H. T. DECANVS

VIRO CLARISSIMO ATQVE DOCTISSIMO

ABRAHAM HESCHEL

VARSOVIANO

POSTQVAM EXAMEN PHILOSOPHIAE RITE SVSTINVIT
ET DISSERTATIONEM LAVDABILEM CVIVS TITVLVS EST

»DAS PROPHETISCHE BEWUSSTSEIN«

AVCTORITATE ORDINIS PROBATAM EDIDIT

PHILOSOPHIAE DOCTORIS
ET ARTIVM LIBERALIVM MAGISTRI

ORNAMENTA ET HONORES

DIE XI. M. DECEMBRIS A. MCMXXXV

RITE CONTVLIT

COLLATAQVE PVBLICO HOC DIPLOMATE

'HILOSOPHORVM ORDINIS OBSIGNATIONE COMPROBATO
DECLARAVIT

*Heschel received his Ph.D. in philosophy from the University of Berlin in 1935, after a
three-year delay because of growing anti-Semitism. (Courtesy of Edward K. Kaplan)*

Abraham Heschel in Frankfurt, Germany (1938), where he relocated to take a position as the director of a Jewish school for adults. (Courtesy of Edward K. Kaplan)

Giving a speech at the Yivo Institute in New York in 1945. Heschel would later publish this speech as a book called The Earth Is the Lord's. (Courtesy of Mrs. Sylvia Heschel)

Heschel (standing, far right) speaking to Prime Minister David Ben Gurion (seated at microphone) and members of the Rabbinical Assembly of America. (Photograph by Rabbi Jacob Segal)

Heschel in his office at the Jewish Theological Seminary, where he taught Jewish studies (1960). (Courtesy of the Ratner Center for the Study of Conservative Judaism)

Heschel with his daughter, Susannah. (Courtesy of Mrs. Sylvia Heschel)

In an effort to heal relations between Catholics and Jews, Rabbi Heschel (center) met with Augustin Cardinal Bea (right) during the Vatican II Summit. (Courtesy of the American Jewish Committee)

Abraham and Sylvia Heschel with Pope Paul VI in Rome. (Courtesy of Mrs. Sylvia Heschel)

Heschel (fourth from left) with Martin Luther King Jr. (center), Ralph Abernathy (third from right), and Rabbi Mordecai Eisendrath carrying Torah in Arlington, Virginia, protesting against the Vietnam War (1968). (Courtesy of Mrs. Sylvia Heschel)

Heschel with his close friend, Rabbi Wolfe Kelman (right), at the Jewish Theological Seminary in 1967. (Courtesy of the Jewish Theological Seminary)

Heschel (right) at Mordecai Kaplan's 90th birthday party. (Courtesy of the Jewish Theological Seminary)

Abraham Joshua Heschel. (Photograph by Lotte Jacobi.
Courtesy of Mrs. Sylvia Heschel)

Teaching rabbinical students at JTS in 1972. (Courtesy of the Jewish Theological Seminary)

Heschel in his office at JTS (1972). (Photograph by Jacob Teshima. Courtesy of Edward K. Kaplan)

Abraham Joshua Heschel, 1907–1972.
(Photograph by Joel Orent. Courtesy of Edward K. Kaplan)

10

Forced Return

"The question about Auschwitz [the Holocaust] to be asked is not, 'Where was God?' But rather, 'Where was man?'"

In 1937, just a few days after celebrating his thirtieth birthday, Abraham moved from Berlin, the capital city of Germany, to Frankfurt. He went there to become the director of a Jewish school for adults. Abraham was to replace Martin Buber, the most famous Jewish teacher in all of Europe, who had recently left Germany for Palestine because of the spread of Nazi hatred. Abraham also wanted to leave Germany, but he had no other job offers at the time. And so Abraham packed his bags for Frankfurt, hoping that he could help the Jews of his new community during this time of pain and sadness. Unfortunately, his efforts would be cut short.

On a cold autumn night in 1938, Abraham lay fast asleep, when in the still darkness he was awakened by a loud knock at the door.

"Abraham Heschel, this is the police. Open the door immediately."

Abraham leaped out of bed, fumbled for his glasses, and rushed to the door. As he turned the doorknob, the Nazi officer kicked the door open and shouted, "All Polish Jews living in Germany are being forced out. You have exactly one hour to pack two suitcases and follow me to the police station. Your train to Poland leaves first thing tomorrow morning."

Alone and frightened, Abraham rushed to pack up his belongings. He then carried two heavy bags to the Frankfurt police headquarters under the watchful eye of the Nazi officer. Abraham was held overnight in a tiny prison cell, and the next morning he was shoved onto an overcrowded train with hundreds of other Polish Jews. The trip home was awful. It took three long days and Heschel was forced to stand for most of the ride. This was certainly not how Abraham wanted to leave Germany.

When the train finally arrived at the Polish border, the local officials refused to admit the Jews. Hitler's influence had already spread to Poland. Abraham and the others were held at the border in miserable conditions. Many people remained there for months, but Abraham was very fortunate; because his family was so well known in Poland, the officials released him after just a few days.

11

A Narrow Escape

*"I am a brand [burning stick] plucked from the fire on
which my people was burned. . . ."*

Back in his hometown of Warsaw, Abraham spent the
next ten months teaching Jewish studies. However, he did
not plan on staying there for very long. He knew that it
would only be a matter of time before the Nazis would
invade his country and terrorize its Jewish communities.
And so, he began applying for jobs in countries as far
from Poland as possible.

In the spring of 1939, Abraham received an invitation to
become a professor at the Hebrew Union College, an
American Jewish university in far-off Cincinnati, Ohio.
Julian Morgenstern, the president of the school, was working very hard to save Jewish teachers from the Nazis. At
first, Abraham didn't want to go because he couldn't take
his family with him. But he soon realized that he would
be more helpful to them in America, where he could speak
directly to other people like Julian Morgenstern, who
might help his family escape from the Nazis.

In the summer of 1939, Abraham left Warsaw for the United States. This would be the last time he would ever see many of his friends, relatives, and his homeland. Just six weeks after he left, the Nazis invaded Poland and destroyed the city of Warsaw and its Jewish community.

12

Alone in America

*"There is an evil which most of us condone [support]
and are even guilty of: indifference to evil.
We remain neutral, impartial, and not easily moved by the
wrongs done to other people."*

Abraham came to America in March 1940, after spending
six months in England with his older brother, Jacob, who
had left Warsaw one year earlier. When he arrived in the
United States, he stayed first with his oldest sister, Sarah,
and her husband in Brooklyn, New York. She was the
only one of Abraham's four sisters to escape from Europe.
Abraham and Sarah were thankful to be reunited. Not
only were they both strangers in a new country, but they
also did not know if they would ever see their other family members again.

In the fall of 1940, Abraham began teaching at the
Hebrew Union College (H.U.C.) in Cincinnati. While he
was grateful to H.U.C. for saving him from the Nazis, his
five years there were very difficult. He was alone in a new
part of the world, and he was also one of the only people
at the college who lived a traditional Jewish lifestyle.

Abraham's greatest challenge was trying to save his mother and sisters from the Nazis. He spoke to American leaders about the viciousness and cruelty of the Nazis; he made public speeches at synagogues and Jewish community centers, and even sent what little money he had back to his family in Poland. Despite all of his efforts, Abraham's mother and three sisters died at the hands of the Nazis. Tragically, he learned of the news while he was alone in Cincinnati.

13

Love, Marriage, and Family

"How much I wish to be in love,
To be close to someone. . . .
Come and take my heart's dearest treasure, my love."

In 1945, as the war in Europe was ending, a ray of light entered Abraham's life. One night, a fellow professor from H.U.C. invited Abraham to his home for a dinner party. Among the guests that evening was Sylvia Straus. Sylvia was a young Jewish concert pianist who had recently come to Cincinnati from her hometown of Cleveland. At the party she was asked to play the piano; her sweet music was soothing to Heschel's troubled soul. Abraham and Sylvia spent the rest of the evening talking. They both enjoyed music, art, and philosophy, and they shared a love of Torah and Jewish life. Over the next few months Abraham and Sylvia fell in love, and they were married in December of 1946. After six lonely years in America, with just a few relatives and friends, Abraham finally had someone with whom he could share his life, in good times and in bad.

The Heschels moved to New York City to start their new life together. Abraham accepted a teaching position at the Jewish Theological Seminary (JTS), the center for Conservative Judaism in North America, and Sylvia continued developing her music career.

In 1952, Abraham and Sylvia had a baby girl, whom they named Hannah Shoshanah (Susannah is her English name). Abraham adored his daughter and loved to play games with her like "red light, green light" and "schoolhouse." As a child he had had no time to play because of his studies, but now as a father he discovered the simple joys of games, toys, and dolls.

When she grew up, Susannah wrote about what it was like to have Abraham Joshua Heschel as her father:

> I remember as a child walking with my father along Broadway, in dirty, noisy, grimy streets, and then turning the corner to go home, walking down the hill toward Riverside Drive, and seeing before us the Hudson River and, sometimes, a magnificent sunset. My father would describe what we were seeing, the wonder of God's miracles in nature, the beauty of a sunset that reminds us of God's presence in the world.

Abraham passed on the teaching of the holy sparks to Susannah, as his parents had passed it on to him. When she grew up, Susannah also became an important teacher of Judaism.

14

Speaker, Writer, Teacher

"What we need more than anything else is not textbooks but textpeople. It is the personality of the teacher which is the text that pupils read, the text that they will never forget."

Abraham spent the next several years teaching and writing books. His first book in English was based on a speech that he gave in New York City in 1946. In this speech, he talked about Jewish life in Europe before the Nazis. Abraham addressed his audience in Yiddish, the language he had spoken as a boy in Warsaw. He mesmerized his listeners with stories about the Ba'al Shem Tov, the Ohev Yisroel, and the holy sparks. His audience was so moved by his words that when he finished, they gave him a standing ovation, and then recited the Kaddish (the special memorial prayer for the dead) together for all the victims of the Holocaust.

When Abraham published this speech as a book, *The Earth Is the Lord's*, he signed it using his full name, Abraham *Joshua* Heschel—the name he was called as a boy in Warsaw. Using his full name made him feel more connected to his family and the European life that had been taken from him.

Within a few years' time, Abraham Joshua Heschel became one of the most well-known religious leaders in North America. He wrote many beautiful books and taught Jews and non-Jews throughout the world about the holy sparks and the need for people to treat each other, and all other living things, with respect and kindness.

In Heschel's most important book, *God in Search of Man*, he said that every child is born with a sense of wonder at the beauty and mystery of the world; this is a feeling that we experience upon seeing a sunset, smelling fresh flowers, or feeling a cool evening breeze. He called this sense of wonder "radical amazement." Heschel explained that what we are experiencing at such moments is God's loving presence in the world. He said that this is God's way of calling on people to work as His partner in completing the work of creation. While many religious teachers have written about the human search for God, Heschel insisted that God is forever searching for us: "God is pursuing man. It is as if God were unwilling to be alone. . . . All of human history as described by the Bible may be summarized in one phrase: God is in search of man."

Heschel spoke of the special role that prayer plays in our attempts to answer God's call, explaining that prayer reminds us of the gifts of life and our responsibility to use these gifts for the good:

We are trained in maintaining our sense of wonder by utter-
ing a prayer. . . . Wishing to eat bread or fruit, to enjoy a
pleasant fragrance or a cup of wine; on tasting fruit in sea-
son for the first time; on seeing a rainbow, or the ocean, on
noticing trees when they are in blossom; on meeting a sage of
Torah or of secular learning; on hearing good or bad things—
we are taught to invoke [mention] God's great name and [to
awaken] our awareness of God.

Another of Heschel's most influential works is a slim
volume called *The Sabbath*. In this book, he describes how
God created the seventh day of the week as a special time
for rest, celebration, and renewal. Using his great skill as a
poet, he calls the Sabbath a "palace in time." Like a palace,
the Sabbath is a special "place in time" where, like members of a royal family, we relax and enjoy the blessings of
friends, family, and nature. Heschel said that the Sabbath
was of particular importance to people in modern times,
who are so busy trying to create new things in the world,
such as computers, satellites, and other technological de-
vices. He explained, ". . . On the Sabbath we are called
upon to . . . turn away . . . from the world of [human] creation [and] to [appreciate God's] creation of the world."

At JTS in New York, Abraham Joshua Heschel also
spent a great deal of his time training young men and
women for careers as leaders in the Jewish community—
rabbis, cantors, and teachers. Although he was often
called away from school to speak with political and religious leaders, Heschel attempted to bring back to his students some of his experiences in the world beyond the
classroom.

One of Heschel's favorite teaching techniques was to
begin his class by sharing with his students a letter he had

recently received from an organization or individual seek-
ing his advice. He would read the letter aloud and then
ask his students for their opinions on the matter.

The following letter came to Rabbi Heschel from the
president of a small synagogue in the Bronx, New York.

> Dear Rabbi Heschel,
> I am writing to ask for your help with an unusual prob-
> lem. After serving the Jewish community in our area for
> several generations, we have decided to close our doors. We
> are doing so because we are no longer needed in this neigh-
> borhood. Almost all of our members have moved to a new
> housing development several miles from our current loca-
> tion, and we will likely reopen our synagogue there in a few
> months time, when we can negotiate for a new space.
> In the meantime, we must sell our current building. At
> present we have two potential buyers, each offering an equal
> amount of money: a Baptist church and a bank. To whom do
> you think we should sell the building?

After reading the letter to his class of rabbinical students, Heschel stroked his beard and asked: "So, gentle-
men, you are all soon to become rabbis, what is your
pesak, what is your Jewish legal decision?"

After a few moments of uncomfortable silence, one student at the back of the room raised his hand and spoke
with confidence: "I recently read an important medieval
book of Jewish law and it stated very clearly that one is
not to sell a synagogue to a church, because Judaism and
Christianity have been rival traditions for so long. There-
fore, my answer is that the people in the Bronx must sell
their building to the bank."

Heschel listened carefully to his eager student, smiled,
and said: "Forgive me if I insult you, but I must disagree.
They may not sell the synagogue to the bank. If it is sold

to the Baptists, it will remain a temple of God; if it is sold to the bank, it will become a temple of money. And a temple of money is no temple at all."

15

In the Footsteps of the Prophets

*"God is to be found in many hearts all over the world.
Not limited to one nation or one people,
[or] to one religion."*

In 1960, while finishing a book about the Hebrew prophets of the Bible—the ancient champions of justice and compassion—Heschel was invited by President Eisenhower to speak at the White House. The President asked for his advice about how best to prepare American schoolchildren to be responsible and caring citizens. Heschel spoke about the importance of teachers serving as role models for children, as he shared with the President his experiences with his uncle Israel and other great teachers from his childhood.

In addition to his concern for American causes, Abraham Joshua Heschel was one of the first religious leaders to stand up for the rights of Jews in the former Soviet Union. In early 1963 he began to speak out against the

Soviet government because it was not allowing Jewish people to practice their religion freely. The government was arresting and punishing people who refused to give up their Jewish heritage. Heschel reminded the American public that just as African Americans were fighting for equal rights in the United States, the Jews of the Soviet Union were fighting for their religious freedom. The only difference was that no one was paying attention to the Soviet Jews: "We are involved in the great battle for equal rights being waged in our country . . . but another drama is being enacted which is agonizing, heart-rending, tragic, and ignored: the plight of the Jews of Soviet Russia."

Heschel insisted that people had to fight for both causes: "The evil of prejudice is indivisible. Discrimination against the political rights of the Negro in America and discrimination against the religious and cultural rights of the Jews in the Soviet Union are indivisible."

In response to Heschel's call to action, many North American Jews began protesting in front of Soviet government buildings, writing letters to their senators and congressmen, and contacting and visiting Jews in the Soviet Union, urging them not to lose hope. Heschel helped launch a campaign that would eventually improve the lives of hundreds of thousands of Soviet Jews.

Heschel also worked hard to bring people of different religions closer together. In 1965, Heschel traveled to Rome, where he met with Pope Paul VI and his assistant, Cardinal Bea, to discuss how to heal relations between Catholics and Jews, who had a long history of bitter fighting. Heschel stated that people of both faiths had to respect the religious choices of the other, without pressuring anyone to change his or her practices or beliefs. In private conversations with the leaders of the church, he insisted that the Catholic Church give up its efforts to convert Jews to Christianity, which had been a part of its philosophy for centuries. Explaining his views on the matter, Heschel said, "I think it is the will of God that there should be religious pluralism [many different religions in the world]." Using an artistic image, Heschel said that without religious diversity, the world would be like a boring museum in which all of the artwork was the same. The Pope listened carefully to Rabbi Heschel and personally changed the official rules of the church because of Heschel's persuasive remarks.

Not all the things that Abraham Joshua Heschel did were popular within the Jewish community or acceptable in the eyes of other religious and political leaders. In 1965, for example, he helped create an organization to protest U.S. involvement in the Vietnam War. Abraham Joshua believed that the country had made a terrible mistake by getting involved in this conflict, and that American soldiers were needlessly killing thousands of innocent citizens in Vietnam. Speaking to a group of students preparing to become priests, he said: " What does God demand of us primarily? Justice and compassion. What does He condemn above all? Murder, killing innocent people."

Many Jewish people thought that Heschel should not speak out against the United States government—even if it was wrong—because the country had been such a helpful friend to Israel. These people feared that if a famous Jewish leader like Abraham Joshua Heschel said something negative about the U.S. government, the friendship between Jews and other Americans, and between the United States and Israel, might be damaged. Heschel strongly disagreed. He believed that real friends have a responsibility to tell each other when they have made a mistake, even when this is hard to do. One of Heschel's most famous statements about the war in Vietnam was, "In a free society, some are guilty, all are responsible." We are all responsible, said Heschel, to make sure that our government acts with a clear sense of justice and compassion in all matters.

16

Heschel and King: Friends and Religious Activists

*"Martin Luther King is a sign that God has not forsaken
the United States of America. God has sent him to us. . . .
I call upon every Jew to hearken to his voice,
to share his vision, to follow his way."*

More than anything else, the American public came to know Abraham Joshua Heschel through his involvement in the African American civil rights movement. In 1963, Heschel gave a powerful speech at a conference in Chicago. He called on people of all races and religions to help African Americans in their struggle for equal rights. Having experienced the terrible pain of being treated like an "outsider" in Nazi Germany, Abraham Joshua was determined to help stamp out racism in his new homeland. With great force, Heschel said that hating people because of the color of their skin was like suffering from "an eye disease." Racism, he insisted, clouds one's ability to see the holy sparks in other people.

It was at this conference that Heschel first met the Reverend Martin Luther King, Jr., the leading figure of the civil rights movement. The two men quickly became close friends and together worked to fight injustice for the next several years. They shared a love of the Bible and the teachings of the prophets, and they both believed that as religious leaders they had a responsibility to stand up for others.

In the winter of 1968, the Jewish Theological Seminary invited Dr. King to speak to its students and faculty in honor of Rabbi Heschel's sixtieth birthday. In his address to this group of Jewish leaders, King said the following of his friend and colleague:

> [Rabbi Heschel] is one of the true great men of our age, a truly great prophet. . . . I remember marching from Selma to Montgomery, how he stood at my side. . . . I remember very well when we were in Chicago for the conference on religion and race. . . . To a great extent, his speech inspired clergymen [religious leaders] of all faiths . . . to do something they had never done before.

When Abraham Joshua returned from the famous Selma march, he wrote in his journal that marching with Dr. King was like walking with one of the great Hasidic masters from his childhood. He said that with every step he took along the streets of Alabama that day, he felt as if his "legs were praying"—praying for a better future for all humankind.

TO PRESIDENT JOHN F. KENNEDY, THE WHITE HOUSE, JUNE 16, 1963

I LOOK FORWARD TO PRIVILEGE OF BEING PRESENT AT MEETING

TOMORROW AT 4 P.M. LIKELIHOOD EXISTS THAT NEGRO PROBLEM WILL BE LIKE THE WEATHER. EVERYBODY TALKS ABOUT IT BUT NOBODY DOES ANYTHING ABOUT IT. PLEASE DEMAND OF RELIGIOUS LEADERS PERSONAL INVOLVEMENT NOT JUST SOLEMN DECLARATION. WE FORFEIT THE RIGHT TO WORSHIP GOD AS LONG AS WE CONTINUE TO HUMILIATE NEGROES. CHURCH, SYNAGOGUES HAVE FAILED. THEY MUST REPENT. ASK OF RELIGIOUS LEADERS TO CALL FOR NATIONAL REPENTANCE AND PERSONAL SACRIFICE. LET RELIGIOUS LEADERS DONATE ONE MONTH'S SALARY TOWARD FUND FOR NEGRO HOUSING AND EDUCATION. I PROPOSE THAT YOU MR. PRESIDENT DECLARE STATE OF MORAL EMERGENCY. A MARSHALL PLAN FOR AID TO NEGROES IS BECOMING A NECESSITY. THE HOUR CALLS FOR HIGH MORAL GRANDEUR AND SPIRITUAL AUDACITY.

Heschel sent this telegram* to President John F. Kennedy in advance of a meeting they had about the African American civil rights movement. He hoped that this letter would move President Kennedy to take swifter and more dramatic action on behalf of the African American community.

*Unlike a regular letter, a telegram does not use full sentences or abide by the usual rules of English grammar.

AFTERWORD

"Remember to build a life as if it were a work of art."

The Torah teaches that Moses, the greatest of all of the Hebrew prophets, left the world with a "kiss from God": in other words, Moses died a peaceful death. Heschel, too, left this world with a kiss. After ushering in the Sabbath with the special Friday evening prayers, enjoying a festive meal, and relaxing with family and friends, he went to bed. Abraham Joshua Heschel passed away in his sleep on December 23, 1972.

On the evening of his death, Heschel had two books on the table by his bed: an old collection of Hasidic teachings and a new book about the Vietnam War. Even in his final hours of life, Heschel continued his quest for justice and compassion by applying the wisdom of his tradition to contemporary events.

After hearing of Dr. Heschel's death, many rabbis, priests, professors, and politicians came to the Heschel home to mourn with Sylvia and Susannah. And at the end of the first month of mourning, thousands of people gathered in synagogues and churches to study Heschel's writings and to tell stories about his legendary life.

Abraham Joshua Heschel dedicated his life to working as God's partner in improving the world by uncovering holy sparks wherever he went. His work as a religious teacher, writer, and activist took him to synagogues, churches, universities, and government agencies around the world. In all of his travels, he spread his message of justice and compassion, touching the hearts and minds of people of different races and religions.

Although Abraham Joshua Heschel, the man, is no longer with us, his memory lives on through the many books he left for us to read and through the efforts of his family, friends, and students, who continue to teach about the hidden sparks. There are also thousands of children in the United States and Canada who study in schools, study societies, and summer camps dedicated to carrying on his legacy.

May Abraham Joshua Heschel's memory continue to be a source of blessing and inspiration—*Yehei zihron barukh.*

GLOSSARY

Hasidim (Cha-see-deem): Hebrew and Yiddish word for "Pious Ones," meaning the followers of the Ba'al Shem Tov. Their central religious belief is that God's presence—"holy sparks"—can be found throughout creation.

Kaddish (Kad-dish): Hebrew name of the traditional memorial prayer for the dead.

kvitelah (kvi-tel-lach): Yiddish word for little notes with prayers on them given by Hasidic Jews to their religious leaders with the expectation that the leaders will pray to God on their behalf.

Mamme (ma-meh): Yiddish word for mother.

neshamah (ne-sha-ma): Hebrew word for spirit or soul.

Ohev Yisroel (O-hev Yees-ra-el): Hebrew for "The One Who Loves the People of Israel"; the nickname given to the first Abraham Joshua Heschel.

rebbe, rebbeim (reb-beh/reb-beyim): Yiddish title(s) given to Hasidic rabbi(s), spiritual leader(s).

Shabbos/Shabbat (Shab-bos/ Shab-bat): Yiddish and Hebrew names for the Sabbath.

Shalom aleikhem (Sha-loem a-lay-chem): Hebrew for "Peace be with you!" a common greeting in traditional Jewish circles.

shteibel (sh-tee-bl): Yiddish word for a small synagogue and study hall.

Tateh (ta-teh): Yiddish word for father.

Torah (To-ra): Hebrew word for the teachings of the Jewish tradition.

tzaddik (tza-deek): Hebrew word for "a righteous person"; used to describe a Hasidic master by his followers.

yeshiva (ye-shee-va): Hebrew and Yiddish word for an academy for traditional Jewish learning.

Zeide (zay-deh): Yiddish word for grandfather or ancestor.

A TIME LINE OF ABRAHAM JOSHUA HESCHEL'S LIFE

1907 Abraham Joshua Heschel is born in Warsaw, Poland.

1925 Leaves Warsaw for Vilna, Lithuania.

1927 Moves to Berlin, Germany, for university studies.

1933 Publishes his book of Yiddish poems, *Der Shem Hame-forash: Mentsch.*

1936 Graduates from the University of Berlin.

1938 Is deported from Frankfurt, Germany, back to Poland.

1939 Leaves Warsaw for the United States, via London, England.

1940 Arrives in the United States and begins teaching at the Hebrew Union College in Cincinnati, Ohio.

1945 Moves to New York to begin teaching at the Jewish Theological Seminary of America.

1946 Marries Sylvia Straus in Los Angeles, California.

1950 Publishes his first book in English: *The Earth Is the Lord's.*

1952 Susannah (Hannah Shoshanah) Heschel, Abraham Joshua and Sylvia's daughter, is born.

1952 Publishes *God in Search of Man.*

1962 Completes his book, *The Prophets,* and is invited to speak at the White House by President Eisenhower.

1963 Attends the Conference on Race and Religion in Chicago, Illinois, where he first meets the Reverend Martin Luther King, Jr..

1965 Marches for African American voting rights with King in Selma, Alabama.

1972 Abraham Joshua Heschel dies at age sixty-five.

INDEX

*Entries followed by page numbers in
boldface refer to photographs.*

and book burning at the
University of Berlin, 22
and family members
deaths, 44
neshamah (caring spirit), 8, 63

O

Ohev Yisroel, 5, 7, 47
definition of, 63

P

Perlow, Israel Shimon, 10
poetry
and birth of a poet, 17–18
and "On the Day of Hate,"
22
Pope Paul VI, 33, 54–55

R

racism, and holy sparks in people, 58
rebbe, definition of, 63
rebbeim, definition of, 63
Reizel, Rivka, *see* Heschel, Rivka
Reizel

S

The Sabbath, 49

Shabbat, definition of, 63
Shabbos, definition of, 63
Shalom aleikhem, definition of, 63
shteibel, definition of, 63
Soviet Union, treatment of Jews
and, 53–54
Straus, Sylvia, *see* Sylvia Heschel

T

Tateh, definition of, 64
Torah, definition of, 64
tzaddik, definition of, 64

V

Vatican II Summit, 33
Vietnam War, and protest of, 34,
55–56
Vilna, and Eastern European
Jewish life, 13–15

Y

yeshiva, definition of, 64
Young Vilna, 17

Z

Zeide, definition of, 64